P9-AQB-875

Getting to Know
CANADA

GETTING TO KNOW

CAN

ADA

REGINA TOR

FOR MOTHER AND DAD
TAK—MERCI

NORTH POLE

GREENLAND

ICELA

ALASKA

BAFFIN BAY

CIRCLE

ARTIC

NORTHWEST TERRITORIES

HUDSON BAY

NO.2 2

NO.1

NO. 4

NO. 3

NO. 5

2

2 2 2

U.S.A.

ATLANTI OCEAN

PACIFIC OCEAN

MEXICO

CUBA

The very word "Canada" is strong and proud. Some say it came from the Iroquois "kanata," which means a cabin or a lodge. Some say it came from the Algonquin "odanah," a settlement. Still others say that the first Spanish sailors, failing to find gold, cried "Aca nada!" or "Nothing of value here!"

Poor Spaniards! How could they have guessed the riches that lay hidden in the wooded hills, beneath the rocks, deep in the sea? Even today man is only beginning to know how great the riches really are. Equipped with new knowledge and modern tools and a restless, imaginative eye, he is drilling and digging deep down into the prairies, into the mountains and valleys and down beneath the ice and snow of the north, under the glacial crust of thousands of years, and he is finding, here in Canada, wealth to dazzle a pirate's eye. But it wasn't a pirate who turned the key in the lock and lifted the lid of this deep and very old treasure chest. It was the bush pilot.

The bush pilot is the hero of modern Canada. He is the pioneer who blazed the trails into the north. Flying "blind" into this vast empty space of no roads and ice-locked rivers, he charted the way for miners and proved to the world that the chest could be opened.

Until 1929 only trappers, missionaries, Eskimos, Indians, a few doctors, a few Mounted Police and a handful of Hudson's Bay Company clerks lived in Canada's north. Then the bush pilot flew in with the mining men. Late in April 1930, two of these men, chipping off samples of rock, found pitchblende —the source of uranium. The day they found it, these miners didn't know it and the world didn't know it, but here on the shores of Great Bear Lake, just south of the Arctic Circle, man had unearthed what is probably the greatest treasure in the whole chest. Uranium is the raw material of atomic energy. Atomic energy is the miracle of power which will one day drive man's trains and planes and ships, heat his homes, do most of his work. So much uranium is being found today in Canada that Canada is rapidly becoming the world's largest producer of this highly precious element.

But uranium isn't the only treasure in the chest. Rich deposits of copper have been discovered in the mountains of the Gaspé and copper is being mined today on the shores of the Arctic Ocean. Iron, a lode larger than the state of Connecticut, is being developed in the unsettled expanses of Labrador and Ungava, and important new discoveries have been made in Ontario. The radium mines by Great Bear Lake are the only supply of radium in all of North America, and gold is still pouring in a steady flow out of Yellowknife.

In 1935 Yellowknife was a settlement of no more than a dozen log huts. Today it is a town of more than 5,000 people—an old established town compared to others in the north. Yellowknife has modern buildings, a theater, a radio station, a shopping district, a social life. Roads and a railway link it with the outside world.

Most towns in the north, though, are newly bulldozed out in the middle of nowhere. These towns owe their lives to the bush pilot who flies in supplies, equipment and men, Christmas mail, schoolbooks, food and medicine. In these towns the younger children have never seen a car or a train. They know only the bush pilot's plane and the dog sled.

Canada's north is wide and varied, and covers almost one third of the nation. To the west, in the territory of Yukon, there are mountains and plateaus cut through with rivers. The Northwest Territories take in all the islands of the Arctic, but the Northwest also has a valley of gardens and fields surrounding the towns that line the banks of the Mackenzie River.

Beyond the towns, up near the North Pole, stretches a chain of weather stations operated jointly by Canada and the United States. From these posts men send out weather reports every three hours to the whole world—important reports which relay information and warnings far in advance of any previously available.

Elsewhere also in Canada things are happening. High up in the Pacific Coast mountains of British Columbia is the huge aluminum project of Kitimat. Kitimat was an engineer's dream that became a reality—a modern drama in five heroic acts. After lumberjacks had cleared a site for a town and bulldozers had dug out roads and helicopters had surveyed the routes for the power lines, the first act began. This was the building of a dam to hold back the waters of a chain of lakes. Next, men dug a ten-mile tunnel into the solid mountain to make a passage for the falling water. When that was done, they built a powerhouse inside the mountain and stretched their transmission lines among the towering snow-topped peaks. Finally and triumphantly they built a monster smelter. Today this smelter is working full blast, making aluminum from bauxite ore. Kitimat is the greatest operation of its kind anywhere in the world. It is a feat that would have daunted even Hercules.

Herculean, too, are the forests in British Columbia. Here a tree rising 200 feet into the air is just another tree, a log eight feet thick is just another log. The world's biggest trucks are used to haul this timber out of the woods and into the water where it begins its journey to the mill. The logs make this trip lashed together into a Davis raft, which is made by tying eighty-foot timbers together to form a frame. The biggest and heaviest logs make the floor, the others are piled on top. As the bottom logs sink, more and more are piled and lashed together until the raft is as high as a two-story house. A tug then tows the raft out to sea, where it begins its often dangerous run to the mill. At the mill the logs are cut into planks and boards for building, most of them going to the United States.

Canada today is cutting all of her forests with care. Trees are harvested as a crop, replaced as they are cut, and protected by rigid government laws. Forests cover more than a third of Canada and make many fathers lumbermen.

Coastal lumberjacks do not look like Paul Bunyan. They are mostly small men, wiry, agile as monkeys and tough as mountain lions. Their life is a rough outdoor life, but they live in neat camps with shower baths and with clean sheets on their beds. In the forest, the lumbermen work swiftly, surely, their cry of "Timber!" before the crashing fall mingling with the whine of saws.

Cutting through the forests and mountains of British Columbia are many swift-running rivers. Some provide electric power for mills and smelting plants. Many are spawning grounds for the fish which provide this province with one of its most important industries. One, the Fraser, has a past as exciting as a wild adventure story.

The Fraser's story is one of gold and of men from as far away as Australia rushing here to get the gold. From the coast they fought their way up to this canyon through 500 miles of wilderness. They came on horseback and they came on foot, dragging their possessions behind them. They fought the Indians, who rolled stones down on them from the cliffs above. Some were massacred, some were drowned in the churning river, but somehow the ones who survived built a road along the sheer-walled canyon and made their way to the gold. Behind the men came pack camels imported from China, lumbering oxen, horses and mules with supplies. By 1862 millions of dollars' worth of gold was moving out of the canyon under armed guards.

In the canyon today a new road replaces the old one. The gold-rush days are gone. Indians fish peacefully in the dark river. Only a few ruined houses and a few old men remain to call forth the ghosts in Jackass Mountain, Stout's Gulch and Antler's Creek. Today, through the canyon, the long trains come and go, swiftly hauling goods across the continent. Above, on the edge of a cliff, cars climb the road to the uplands.

In the uplands lies the rolling range of the Dry Belt, the land of ranches and cattle, sheep and stallions and Indian cowboys. Beyond the brown range stretch a ragged line of mountains and the sky.

The mountains of British Columbia are lean-ribbed and tall, with sharp crags and rough edges—beautiful, majestic mountains holding clear lakes in cuplike hollows. Here live bighorn sheep and nimble goats, moose, antelope and grizzly bears.

British Columbia is impressive because so much of it is mountains. Only along the coast does the land grow quiet and flatten out like a path beside the Pacific. Lining this path, from Vancouver in the south all the way to Alaska, are busy pulp mills and large fish canneries and the beginnings of new projects. Off the coast, the sea teems with fish—salmon, halibut, herring and cod. Farther out swim whales, seals, porpoises and sea otters. On the beach, the tides of the ocean leave delicious shellfish, and all along the coast stretches the dark forest with its thick undergrowth of ferns, flowers, mosses and wild berries.

In British Columbia there are two Vancouvers—the city and the island. If you look at the map, you will see that the city is built on the shore of the mainland. The island acts as a shield between the city's harbor and the rough waters of the Pacific.

From a small sawmill called Gas Town, Vancouver sprouted almost overnight into a glittering city of wealth, grace and beauty. Today Vancouver is the third largest city in the nation. Here, surrounded by water and towering blue-green mountains, live one half of all the people in British Columbia.

VANCOUVER ISLAND
VICTORIA • VANCOUVER

NO. 1

Victoria, the capital of British Columbia, perches above a beach on the southeastern tip of Vancouver Island. Long ago Victoria became known as Canada's Garden of Eden and the city has always made sure it kept its English hedges pruned, its roses blooming in December, its tea in the garden, and holly and boar's-head for Christmas. Today retired teachers from Vermont, pensioned engineers and railway conductors from Ontario, Czechs, Chinese, Frenchmen and South Americans have turned this English Eden into an international retirement city.

Back of Victoria and the cultivated rolling green hills, Vancouver Island is wild and, like so much of Canada, mostly uninhabited. With thick forests and mountains topped with snow, the island follows the mainland for nearly 300 miles.

Completely different from the Pacific Coast is the Atlantic Coast. Here mountains are smaller, more rounded, and trees are shorter and thinner. As in our country, the first settlers in Canada came across the Atlantic from Europe. There are no written records of the earliest days when Leif Ericson and his Norsemen first sighted Canada's coast. That was nearly 1,000 years ago. From the time of John Cabot, though, we have many stories, most of them about the uncounted millions of cod swimming in the cold sea. After Cabot came Jacques Cartier, who founded New France when he planted a cross on the shores of the Gaspé. Cartier also discovered the St. Lawrence, the long deep-water highway that leads straight into the heart of North America.

NEWFOUNDLAND

LABRADOR

GANDER

ST. JOHN'S

NEW
BRUNSWICK

P.E.I.

CAPE
BRETON

NOVA SCOTIA

SAINT JOHN

HALIFAX

★ CHARLOTTETOWN

NO.2

For many years settlement in Canada was slow, for this was wild country. What are known today as the Atlantic Provinces (Nova Scotia, New Brunswick, Newfoundland and Prince Edward Island) were settled first, and in many ways they are like four old sea captains. These four have always lived by and from the sea, taking great quantities of cod, herring, tuna, salmon, lobster and other fish from the gray-green ocean, building ships for trade and transport, and receiving in their harbors all kinds of goods from other lands to distribute throughout Canada.

Nova Scotia, which has a shape like a lobster, was founded first by the French. Later there were more Scots than Frenchmen here. They called this province New Scotland because it looked like home. Many Nova Scotians are farmers raising livestock and growing field crops. Their farms are tiny and old dikes built long ago still hold back the sea. Along the coast little towns nestle in coves between the rocks and send their men to sea to fish, remembering with pride their days of wealth and great shipbuilding. Three quarters of Nova Scotia is forest land, where many fathers work at lumbering, and back in the hills there are pulpwood mills, and important mines which provide Canada with much of its coal. In the southwest, the apple trees in Annapolis Valley blossom pink and white for eighty miles in late May.

The Scots cling staunchly to Scottish ways. Today the young people do not speak Gaelic, the language of old Scotland, but the old ones still do and it is sometimes on the tongues of miners and lonely fisherfolk drying cod on the beaches below the rocks.

During the American Revolution, 35,000 Loyalists (Americans who were still loyal to the British Crown) left the Thirteen Colonies and came into Nova Scotia and New Brunswick. They took to this country, for it was something like their own New England, and they, with all the others, have contributed much to the building of Canada.

The capital of Nova Scotia is Halifax. Running down a hill, Halifax thrusts long piers, like teeth on a big comb, far out into the harbor, and the sea in turn pokes long fingers up into the heart of the city. Halifax is one of the world's busiest ports and one of the oldest in the Western Hemisphere. In and out of her harbor have come and gone all kinds of ships—pirate ships and smugglers, battleships and mercy ships and always the steady ships of trade and fish. During the winter Halifax is particularly busy. With the St. Lawrence frozen tightly shut, Halifax and Saint John in New Brunswick handle all of Canada's Atlantic Ocean trade.

Saint John is New Brunswick's principal city. Saint John is ancient and dignified, but Saint John is also a cheerful, bustling, foggy international deep-sea port and a busy industrial city. Here sugar from the West Indies is refined. Tea, coffee, and spices are unloaded from the holds of foreign ships and packaged and sent out again to fill the grocery shelves across Canada. Fish is processed in huge quantities, many cans of cod and salmon ending up in America's supermarkets. Logs are beaten into pulp for paper. Raw cotton coming in is woven into textiles and together with other goods is shipped across a thousand miles into central Canada.

Geographically speaking, it would be easier to ship these goods down into Maine, but easy geography has had very little to do with the making of any part of Canada. The same mountains that heap their hills through our eastern states push their way up through the Atlantic Provinces. Great deposits of soft coal in these mountains make miners out of many fathers, particularly on Cape Breton Island, where the seam of coal is wide and deep. Cape Breton also has a very important iron and steel industry.

In many ways Nova Scotia looks Scotch, but New Brunswick wears an English face. Wood is the great crop of this country. Many rivers and valleys wind between the wooded hills, and all through the country, as in Nova Scotia, stand textile mills and fish-canning plants and pulpwood mills. From these and all the other pulpwood mills in Canada, rolls and rolls of newsprint are shipped out every year to the States.

Nestling into the curve of New Brunswick and Nova Scotia is the "Garden of the Gulf." This is Prince Edward Island. Tiny, sweet-climated Prince Edward has no industry, just farms stretching from one tip to the other, the rich loam growing potatoes and fruits. Charlottetown, the capital, is the historic site where Canadians first gathered to discuss the idea of Canada as a nation—the idea that became reality in 1867.

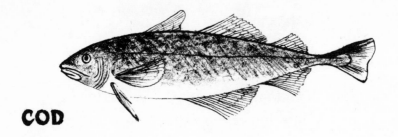

COD

Newfoundland is Canada's newest province. It became part of the nation in 1949. Until recently, cod fishing was the most important industry, supporting at least one half of all the people. Since the war, thriving new towns have developed on this rocky, wind-whipped island along with an increasingly important pulp and paper industry. More and more men today are also going into the hills to mine the almost untouched riches of coal, lead, zinc, copper and iron. Newfoundland is the place where men mine for iron also under the sea—a strange-sounding idea but actually practical.

Labrador, the vast mainland portion of Newfoundland, although mostly unexplored and very sparsely inhabited, contains one of the richest deposits of iron ever uncovered by man.

Since World War II, the great airfield at Gander has become a global crossroads and has given a new importance to Newfoundland. Twenty-four hours a day, diplomats, movie stars, army men, and refugees from many countries arrive and depart at Gander.

The people of Newfoundland came here long ago, in the days of Queen Elizabeth. In some of the outlying villages, which perch like gulls on the cliffs above the sea, people still sing songs that were sung in Shakespeare's time, and the towns they live in wear names like Heart's Content and Seldom-Come-By.

As the early fishermen of Europe came to Newfoundland, they also came to the Gaspé Peninsula. Today the Gaspé is part of Quebec but the people are still Gaspésians and cod is still king. War brought a new prosperity—tourists, a greatly developed lumber industry, the discovery of copper, and the hope of oil in the rugged hills. For most of the people, however, life is still lived out in the tiny villages and fields. Designs for fishing boats which the original French settlers brought with them in the 1600's, are still used today. The only change made by present Gaspésians is the addition of a Diesel engine. Bread is still baked in outdoor ovens and handicrafts still fill the leisure hours. Handwoven textiles, rugs and linens are made by women and girls. Wood carving is the ancient art of men and boys.

BREAD
PADDLE

The northern coast of the Gaspé is a land of steep cliffs, a wild and ragged coastline where gannets and gulls dive for food, and houses cling precariously, just out of reach of the sea. The southern coast is much more gentle with meadows turning white with daisies in July. The interior is all mountains covered with thick forests which are almost impassable—in summer with their dense undergrowth and in winter with twenty feet of snow.

Quebec is Canada's largest province. Quebec's first settlers were French, and French is the language spoken most often here. French is also one of the two official languages of Canada. In Quebec "Mister" becomes "Monsieur"; "Mother," "Mère"; and "Father," "Père." Along country roads stand wayside shrines, and along the St. Lawrence farm fields run in narrow strips up from the river's edge.

In the villages some of the old houses look like those in the north of France—stone houses, long and low, with fat chimneys at either end. Many are made of wood, with weathered shingles and blue roofs. Some are gaily painted red, pink, blue or yellow, with potted plants in white lace-curtained windows. Against the house leans the woodpile for the big-bellied stove in the kitchen. In the yard grow flowers and vegetables, the tobacco patch for Monsieur's pipe. In winter these villages are drifted with snow and busy with horse-and-sleighs, bobsleds loaded with logs, and children snowshoeing home from school. At suppertime the narrow streets are empty and white and still. In warm, good-smelling kitchens big families sit around the table spooning up the thick pea soup, contented. Outside, in the cold stillness, the church bell rings.

In rural towns the *curé* (the priest) and his church are the center of life. "Monsieur le curé" is the real leader of the French-Canadian people, for he is wholly of them and with them always. From the earliest days when priests were explorers, and missionaries were martyred by hostile Indians whom they sought to teach and convert, the curés have guided and taught and consoled the people of Quebec.

In many Quebec schools nuns and priests teach the classes. In many hospitals sisters tend the sick. In some areas Trappist monks have opened up the land and taught the farmers how to grow good crops. Up in the Lake St. John district it was the Trappists who started the blueberry-canning industry. You can see them in the fields, their straw hats and white robes bent above the green bushes, pruning, hoeing and harvesting bumper crops.

All through the southern part of Quebec the unbelievably blue Laurentian Mountains seem to form a backdrop for the tiny villages, the farms, the rolling green hills. For centuries the French-Canadian countryman has worked this soil. He loves it with a deep and abiding love, and in his children he has instilled this same emotion. When he could afford to send his sons to school, he urged them to become doctors, lawyers, teachers or priests—members of the learned professions. Then World War II came. Materials were desperately needed and smoking chimneys rose rapidly between the church spires up and down the St. Lawrence. Factory whistles blew shrill and sharp, calling the young people of Quebec to a new kind of school. Quickly now, machines and industrial science had to be learned. More and more men were needed for the ever-increasing number of factories, research plants and mills. With the same fervor they showed long ago in exploring this continent, French Canadians quickly became expert technicians. Since the end of the war, Quebec has kept on expanding her industries. Today she leads all other provinces in technical education.

Quebec City, the only walled city in North America, is built upon a rock rising straight up out of the St. Lawrence. Tier on tier, the towers, buttresses, spires and steeples seem to pierce the sky, and lights at night twinkle like a thousand tiny candles on a dark altar.

It was 1608 when Champlain built his first frail fort at the foot of the rock, and 1620 when he built his second one at the top. These beginning years were years of barter and trade in furs, of Indians howling at the walls, and long, hungry winters when the supply ships from France didn't come—years when the settlers, far from the gentle fields of France, looked out at a wild and untamed land and prayed. Later there were years when the city lived like a gay lady, with silks and satins and plumed hats, banquets and duels and romantic gallantry. And finally there was the year of disaster.

It was a warm June day in 1759 when the thirty-two-year-old British general, James Wolfe, led his men ashore and stole up the hill to the Plains of Abraham. There he and the great French general, Montcalm, met and fought and died. Quebec had fallen to the English, but Quebec has always been and perhaps will always remain French.

Built of gray stone and mortar, half of the city rests beside the river. This is Lower Town—narrow cobbled streets, old houses, churches, chimney pots, cats and dogs and calling children. On the plateau above sits Upper Town with its old gray-stone houses shuttered and mysterious and hiding old romantic stories behind walled gardens. Between the two towns narrow streets climb and wind their way up the steep cliffs lined with buildings wedged deep in the rock. Most people who go by foot today use the funicular.

The modern business streets are as modern as they are in any city. Only the market remains as it has always been. Here in the open square, chickens, ducks, pork, mutton, vegetables and fruits are laid out in open carts. The air is filled with the mingling smells, filled with the cries of bargaining housewives and children impatient to go home. In another square, the *calèches*, the black carriages with high white wheels and single well-groomed horses, wait for fares. Cabbies snooze and birds peck among the cobblestones for grains from the horses' nose-bags.

Beyond the city, back up from the river, Quebec the Province is still the country of *Alouette* and of ancient pure-French songs. Songs like *Sur le Pont d'Avignon* have been sung by these people since the first *voyageurs* paddled the dark, unknown rivers.

North of the St. Lawrence Valley lies a giant horseshoe-shaped stretch of land extending from Labrador in the east all the way over to Lake Winnipeg in the west. This is the Canadian Shield. From Lake Winnipeg it sweeps north through the prairie provinces to the Arctic Ocean. The Shield is a vast undulating plateau covered with noble forests of spruce and pine and threaded with thousands of lakes, rivers and bogs. Deep within the ancient rocks lie rich deposits of iron, gold, silver, nickel, copper, platinum, cobalt and uranium. Trappers, traveling by canoe, bring out of the forest precious furs—beaver, otter, muskrat, mink, ermine, marten and lynx. Canoes, invented by the Indians, are still used, for the rivers are rough with rapids and there are no roads, no trains—only planes that fly between marked destinations. Here in the Shield men are lumberjacks, miners and trappers, strong and hardy, raising the rafters on Saturday night with their lusty songs, isolated far from the lights of cities, working to make Canada grow.

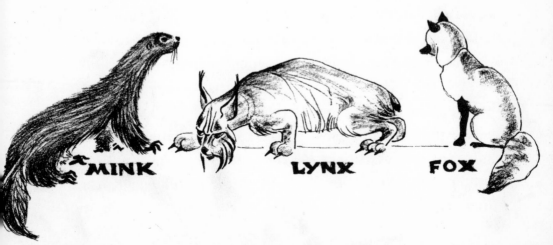

MINK   LYNX   FOX

The Shield extends over most of Quebec and provides this province with the raw materials for her many industries. Thousands of maple trees yield sugar and syrup, much of which goes to stores in the States. Mills turn out textiles. Leather and rubber-goods factories smell up the air. The many swift-flowing rivers provide power for pulp-and-paper mills and smelting plants, Quebec's leading industries. In the southernmost part of the province are the largest deposits of asbestos in the world. The uses of asbestos are so many—all the way from parts of battleships to pot holders—and the world is so hungry for this material, that asbestos has become a many-million-dollar-a-year industry in Canada.

More than half of all Canada's people make their homes on the gently sloping plain that spreads across southern Quebec and Ontario. They earn their livings on the farms, in the orchards, in the factories of thriving industrial cities and in the metropolitan areas of Montreal, Toronto and Ottawa.

Canada's largest city is the Quebec city of Montreal, which is built around a mountain on a green island in the middle of the St. Lawrence. It was from Montreal that the first explorers went out to open the gates of this continent—LaSalle forging south to the Mississippi, Cadillac west to establish the first trading post on the site of Detroit, and Alexander Mackenzie with heroic bravery pushing through the forbidding Rockies down to the Pacific Ocean.

Later, following in Mackenzie's footsteps, went the railroad builders to tie the country together with their long tracks of steel, and these men too left from Montreal.

Although Montreal is located 1,000 miles from the ocean, it is a seaport, one of Canada's most important. Ocean-going vessels, naval craft, icebreakers, long grain freighters, river, lake and coast carriers and small, strong tugs choke the canals and fill the air with their sea smells and wonderful hooting sounds of work. In among the shipyards loom large grain elevators and cold-storage warehouses for the furs, fresh-water fish and other foods pouring in from the interior of Canada.

NO.4

Just after the St. Lawrence leaves Lake Ontario it separates the province of Ontario from the state of New York. Ontario has a shape somewhat like a giant's leg, fat and bulging in spots. The foot of this leg juts deep down into the United States and is the only part of Canada that resembles the industrial regions of the States. Here are Windsor, twin automobile city of Detroit; the big steel mills at Hamilton; Chatham, Oshawa, London—all the big names of industry which produce the machines, the tools, the equipment required by a great industrial nation. Yet, just beyond the smoking factories are rich cornfields, tomato and tobacco fields, dairy farms, apple and peach orchards and vineyards, old brick farmhouses and sweeping elms.

On the heel of Ontario's foot sits Ottawa, capital of the nation. Ottawa was originally Bytown, a rip-roaring lumberjack's town. Here, high above a trio of rivers, in the imposing gray-stone Parliament buildings, the laws of the nation are made. Canada is a democracy, but Canada does not have a President. Canada has a Governor-General, who is appointed by Her Majesty the Queen upon recommendation of the Prime Minister, and a Prime Minister, who is the leader of the political party with the largest number of members in the House of Commons. The Governor-General must give his consent to all laws passed by Parliament before they can go into effect, but the Prime Minister has the real power. The House of Commons, together with the Senate, makes up Parliament. Members of the House are elected by the people. Senators are appointed for life by the government.

THE CANADA GOOSE

Toronto is the capital of Ontario. Toronto is also the book-publishing and national-magazine center of Canada, an important banker financing many of the new explorations in the north, and an important center of commerce and culture. The University of Toronto is the largest in Canada and is noted for its high academic standing.

In Canada, when the geese fly south in the fall, the school bells ring and everywhere across the land children sit again at desks with newly sharpened pencils, a new dress for the first day. Some of the schools are modern, glass-walled buildings. Some are one- and two-room country schools. Even the log schoolhouse of pioneer days can still be seen in some places where only a few children live. On the prairies, children from wide-spaced farms go by bus to big consolidated schools. In Quebec, children and teachers speak French, books are written in French, and religion is studied along with history, geography, English and math. To all schools, however, no matter where they are, go special radio programs prepared by the Canadian Broadcasting Corporation and films made by the National Film Board. These programs bring to life the subjects studied in books and help to make school fun.

All Canadian children must attend school until they are sixteen. Education, however, is not limited to schools. Adult education and correspondence courses enrich the lives of many young people and adults and bring the world closer to city dwellers as well as to winter-lonely fishermen and farm people, and to families in isolated towns in the new north. Business schools, agricultural schools, music and art schools—there are all kinds for anyone wanting to learn.

All classes, of course, are stopped during the year by many holidays. At Christmas the tree is trimmed with tinsel and balls and colored lights. Easter brings the bunny with his basket of decorated eggs. Thanksgiving, which comes in October, means feasting and family reunions. And then there are days important in Canadian history, like Dominion Day on the first of July and the Queen's birthday, which are also celebrated as holidays.

Canadians, children and adults both, play a great variety of games—baseball, football, volleyball, ice hockey, soccer, tennis and many others. Ice hockey is Canada's national sport and everyone from grandfather down to the youngest child is a fan. Canadian ice-hockey teams have an international reputation, as do Canadian skiers, skaters and bobsledders.

INTERNATIONAL
SNOWSHOER'S
CONVENTION
•
SNOWSHOE RACES,
PARADES, SOCIAL
EVENTS TO PER-
PETRATE TRADITION
OF "COUREUR
DE BOIS"

Children take to skis and skates almost as soon as they can walk, and snowshoes in some places are standard equipment for getting to school. Families skate together on winter Sunday afternoons, or pile into the big sleigh for a gay, bell-jingling ride over the frozen hills. Fun is mixed with work when the maple trees are tapped in the spring. Summer is corn and wiener roast time, picnics, canoe trips, the camp in the woods.

Canada has many national and provincial parks—wonderful vacation areas which are also sanctuaries for buffalo, caribou, elk, deer, moose and bear —all the animals that once roamed freely here. In wooded and unsettled regions all of these animals and more can still be found. The unlucky ones provide meat for the hunter and fur for the trapper. In Canada's lakes and rivers live many kinds of waterfowl and fish.

Autumn brings agricultural fairs—the judging of cattle and hogs, chickens, pies, jellies, and jams; the ox-pulling contests, the harness races, the Ferris wheel and spinning games of chance.

All during the year, young people practice for the annual regional and provincial music festivals which offer prizes and scholarships to outstanding young artists. The Canadian Broadcasting Corporation also does much to encourage music. Over its three major networks, one in French, go concerts by symphony orchestras, choirs, school glee clubs, instrumental groups and folk singers.

The CBC is playing an important role in the building of Canada, where towns and cities are separated by such great distances. Peoples in the various provinces meet each other rarely, but through the CBC, Canadians are learning to know Canadians. Almost every family, no matter how isolated, owns a radio and is linked by it to the world.

Not only radios, but telephones, refrigerators, washing machines—most of the "conveniences of life"—are found today in many Canadian homes. The majority of Canadians live much as Americans live. They even use many of the same products, look at the same TV programs and read the same magazines. In fact, if you took just a casual glance, if you didn't stop to speak to the people, you probably couldn't tell an American from a Canadian.

Canadians, however, are distinctly themselves—a combination of British, French and North American peoples and cultures. They are at the same time both daring and conservative. They are realistic, for they believe in doing what is practical rather than talking about what might be perfect. They are hard workers and their way of working is Americanlike, with efficient assembly-line production and mass-scale business. They are, above all, a young nation full of hope with the promise of their future.

CANADA

Canada became a nation with the passage of the British North America Act in 1867, but it wasn't until the first transcontinental train started moving between Montreal and the Pacific that the written word became a reality. The train carried men from the east to settle the west, and then brought the harvests back out of the west to feed the east and a big part of the rest of the world. The train spanned the wide spaces and tied all of the parts together as one. The train was the first miracle that made possible all the succeeding miracles in the exciting story of Canada.

Winter comes to Canada with the wind from the north—a great swirling wind in a slate-gray sky. And with the wind comes the snow, driving across the prairie, sifting down through the streets of Ontario's towns and piling great white drifts against the doors of Quebec. In the woods, snow-silent now, sleighs carry logs to the rivers, where they will be piled and left to wait for spring. Out along the Atlantic, snow blurs the harbors and big white-fingered icicles hang on the riggings of ships. In the Rockies, moose, deer and rabbits leave their footprints in the deep, soft snow. Everywhere mountains turn blue-white with cold. Only along the coast of British Columbia does winter forget to be fierce. Melting away to fog and rain, winter lies down in the pockets of Victoria's little hills and falls asleep.

On the prairies, where winter often plunges the thermometer way below zero, the earth is rich and the farms are big. Neighbor cannot call to neighbor—he is too far away. But a man can see for long distances because there is no hill to stop his eye. Once buffalo grounds, the prairie today is a wide space of golden grain broken here and there by tall oil derricks.

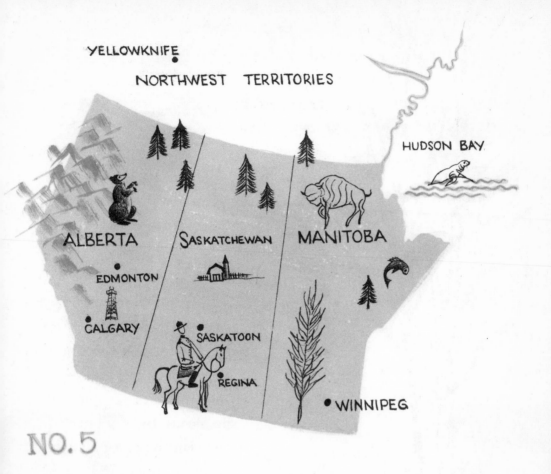

YELLOWKNIFE
•
NORTHWEST TERRITORIES

HUDSON BAY

ALBERTA   SASKATCHEWAN   MANITOBA

EDMONTON
•

CALGARY
•   SASKATOON
              •

              REGINA
              •

                                    • WINNIPEG

NO. 5

The prairie provinces (Manitoba, Alberta and Saskatchewan) were built by people of many lands—by Russians, Ukrainians, Germans, Norwegians, Swedes, Poles, Icelanders and Dutch, by restless men from eastern farmlands and by the Scots who settled here first. Many of these people, while building this, their new country, have retained the traditional holidays and church rites, the songs, stories and dances of their native lands. Their customs, their ways of life, are woven into the fabric of Canada. Their part in the building of Canada has helped to make this country grow.

Since the Second World War, great numbers of Europe's people are again crossing the Atlantic and entering Canada's welcoming door. Canada welcomes these people because she needs them. There is so much land here, so much wealth in forest, mine and farmland still untouched, that without these New Canadians, Canada could never hope to fulfill her tremendous promise of greatness. Scientists, farmers, teachers, industrial workers, artists and musicians, these New Canadians are building the nation ever stronger as they come with new ideas and new skills.

Winnipeg, the capital of Manitoba, is typical of the contributions made by these people of many lands. In the middle of the prairie they planted trees, made parks, built tall business buildings, fine homes and a university—a truly modern city. Winnipeg's Grain Exchange is one of the world's largest markets for the sale of grain. Winnipeg is also a transportation center, and from modern meat-packing plants large quantities of beef and pork products are shipped out across the nation.

WHEAT

On the streets a dozen languages can be heard in a single day, and the talk reveals that these are world-minded people. The man who grows the wheat and sees it hauled away to markets in distant lands is a world-minded man because when anything happens to close off his markets, he suffers. The prairie man cares what is going on in the rest of the world because he knows better than most that what happens elsewhere directly affects his life.

Markets and water. These two spell life or death, poverty or riches, in the prairies. The amount of rain here in June and July determines how much bread men in far-off lands will eat the following spring. By the same token, if the wheat is stunted by drought, the prairie man's daughter doesn't go back to college. Complete failure of the crops means disaster. Children go hungry. Machines go unrepaired. A man returns his car to the dealer, unable to pay, and this in turn means that men working on the assembly line back east in the automobile city of Windsor will be on relief before next spring. Wheat is so all-important that the whole of Canada is affected by the crop.

There have been bad years on the prairies, years of drought and grasshoppers and rust on the wheat—hard years. But this is the country of perpetual hope, and belief that the land will always come back, that next year's crop will be the best yet. Strangely enough, the land always has come back. In the meantime, though, the prairie man has learned to raise cattle and hogs for the meat-packing industry in Winnipeg, to raise oats and barley in addition to wheat. Government experimental farms work tirelessly to develop new types of wheat not affected by rust, wheat which will ripen earlier and make an even better loaf of bread.

In spite of hardships, life on the prairies is good. This is a friendly place wide-open to the sky, the place where neighbor helps neighbor and winter becomes the "curling" time for men.

Curling, called a "roarin' game," came straight from Scotland. Players slide heavy stones across an ice-floored rink somewhat as bowlers throw their balls. Team members with brooms frantically sweep the ice in front of the stone as it goes, trying to increase its speed and control its direction. Banker, minister, farmer—almost every man is an avid player and an ardent fan. In recent years, curling has spread across the continent, some Canadian teams playing in competition with American teams.

When winter comes, some farm families move into town until spring seeding time. The men curl, talk world politics and wheat. The women forget their farm chores, go to the movies, play bridge, and talk wheat too, just because they can't help it.

Saskatoon, a friendly, leisurely city in the province of Saskatchewan, abounds with wheat growers during the winter months. The university here is well-known for its research center dedicated to the peaceful uses of atomic energy. The province of Saskatchewan is a leading producer of uranium ore, which is found in the north along with rich forests and an important lumbering industry. Many Saskatchewan farmers keep horses, cattle and sheep, shipping dairy products, beef and wool to markets in the east. This province also has great spouting oil wells and, in the south, important beds of coal.

The other two prairie provinces are equally important. Manitoba, roughly the size of France, has in addition to its wheat farms in the south, rich mines of gold, copper, zinc and nickel. The northern half of this province is part of the Shield, thinly settled but providing Manitoba with important minerals, lumber and furs. Many rivers and large lakes make fishing also an important industry.

Alberta, bounded by the Rocky Mountains in the west, is the largest of the Prairie Provinces. Alberta has tremendous oil fields and vast resources of natural gas and coal. Cattle ranches in the foothills of the Rockies gave birth to the annual wild-and-woolly Calgary Stampede. Each year thousands of people come to Calgary to watch the bronco "busted," Indians dance, the cowboys rope and tie their steers. Edmonton, the capital, is the oil center of Canada, the gateway to the north, the place where the Alaska Highway begins.

Regina, the capital of Saskatchewan, was originally an Indian campsite called Pile of Bones. Later it became a Royal Northwest Mounted Police post. Today it is training headquarters for the Royal Canadian Mounted Police.

The red-coated Mountie works hard and to the Eskimos of the far north he is many things. He is their postmaster, sorting mail, handing out family allowance checks and old-age pensions. He registers births and deaths. He takes the census, he enforces fur and game laws, and he is often doctor and nurse, the only comfort when emergencies are sudden and help is air-miles away across the frozen tundra.

The Arctic, of course, isn't all frozen tundra. We used to think it was an unfriendly and unlivable place, but we know now this isn't true. In some places wild strawberries, cranberries, dandelions and other flowers grow in thick, knee-high carpets. In summer, in some areas, flies and mosquitoes pester the Eskimo just as much as they do you.

Until recently, the coming of the white man did little to change the Eskimo's ways. Seals and caribou have always provided him with most of his needs — food, clothing, fuel, light and shelter. Canvas tents have replaced the seal tents for summer living in most places, but the igloo is still the winter home. Today Eskimos import their summer clothes through mail-order houses or sew them on portable sewing machines. Caribou skins are still used for winter clothes, for if an Eskimo is poorly clad he can't go far from home or stay out long enough to hunt for food.

The Eskimo is a very creative man. He lives where there are few raw materials, yet he has invented an amazing number of things. Not only tents, canoes and tailored clothes of skins, but combs and buttons of ivory, dog sleds, snowshoes, goggles to protect his eyes from the glare of ice, games and toys for his children, lamps, spoons, pipes and tools—all these he has made. From earliest times Eskimos have been excellent carvers, and today they are learning that their handicrafts are bringing good prices in the markets farther south. Their figures of animals, birds and people are prized works of art, full of individuality and spirited charm.

The Eskimo's world today is changing. Young men are found in the armed forces, some in the government, some in college preparing to teach, some training as technicians for

Arctic weather stations. Only with the Eskimo's help can Canada develop the Arctic, which is so important to the whole North American continent.

Unlike the Eskimos, the Indians of Canada are found scattered throughout the country. Some live on "reserves." Others live in the general community. Among the Indians are widely differing physical characteristics and ways of living. On the Pacific Coast, descendants of the early salmon fishermen are still active in the fishing industries. In the interior of British Columbia many earn their living as fruit farmers, ranchers and lumbermen. On the prairies, the sons of the buffalo hunters are now ranchers and grain growers. Along the St. Lawrence, the Iroquois and the Algonquins are found on the farms, in the factories, in the cities as doctors, teachers, and workers at many different kinds of jobs. In the Atlantic Provinces they fish and farm and work in the forests.

In certain areas the traditional arts of basket weaving and wood carving provide full-time jobs for both men and women. These arts have had a definite influence on Canada and together with the Indians' stories and songs have helped to make "Canadian art."

Completely different from the arts of all other North American Indians are the totem poles, the enormous houses built of wood and the great war canoes which belonged to the Indians of British Columbia. The totem poles, which are monumental sculptures in cedar, were actually family coats of arms. Ravens, eagles, bears, wolves and other animals and fish were the favorite motifs. Totemism was the belief that ancestors, disguised as animals, were sacred. They ruled the family ceremonial life.

Many peoples, many ways of life, have gone into the making of Canada. It is truly a multi-colored fabric, woven together and made complete by a central democratic government. Although Her Majesty the Queen of England is also Queen of Canada, the Queen does not rule. She is a symbol in Canada of ancient British traditions. Canada's system of government is actually very much like that of the United States. A federal government takes care of all matters of national concern, and the country is divided into ten provinces and two territories. The provinces make laws governing education and all other matters of provincial concern. The two territories of Yukon and the Northwest, because they have so few people, are administered by the federal government.

When North America was first being settled, relations between Canada and the United States were not always friendly. The beginning years were often bitter years marked with fighting and fear. Today, sharing the same continent, exchanging peoples and ideas, the two countries have learned a lesson from which the whole world can benefit. Canada and the United States today are close neighbors who have learned to live as friendly neighbors, their boundary line "unfenced," a line that can be crossed freely in either direction without need even of passport.

Canada, so full of promise, so young and strong and rich with treasures yet to be explored, wears its name like a song— Canada.

HISTORY

About 1000 years ago: Leif Ericson believed to have reached the Atlantic.

1497: John Cabot sighted Newfoundland and possibly Cape Breton.

1534: Jacques Cartier, a Breton explorer, landed at Gaspé Harbor and discovered the St. Lawrence River.

1608: First permanent settlement, Quebec, founded by Champlain. It became the base for French expansion.

1759: Battle of Plains of Abraham, Quebec.

1763: Treaty of Paris. French ceded territory in what is now Canada to Great Britain.

1774: Quebec Act gave French traditions a permanent security.

1791: Constitutional Act gave Upper and Lower Canada (roughly the present Ontario and Quebec) each a Lieutenant Governor and a legislature.

1840: Act of Union joined Upper and Lower Canada.

1867: British North America Act passed by the Parliament of Great Britain.

1869: Canada bought vast territory of northwest from Hudson's Bay Company. From this the prairie provinces were created—Manitoba in 1870, Saskatchewan and Alberta in 1905.

1871: The Pacific colony, British Columbia, joined the Confederation; in 1873 and 1949 the maritime provinces, Prince Edward Island and Newfoundland, joined.

1931: Statute of Westminster passed by British Parliament. Canada, and other self-governing nations of the British Empire, recognized as autonomous members of the Commonwealth of Nations.

1945: Canada actively participated at San Francisco in drafting the charter of the United Nations. Since, Canada has been a very active member of the U.N.

1949: After participating in the initial discussions, Canada was one of the nations who signed the Atlantic Treaty.

INDEX

SOURCES

Fifty-four sources, including books, pamphlets and periodicals, as well as bulletins, and reports from the Canadian governments have been used to prepare this text. The author extensively used films loaned by the National Film Board of Canada, and to Ralph Ellis she expresses her sincere appreciation.

The Canadian Information Division, Department of External Affairs, Ottawa, can provide additional helpful material. For further reading, the following available books and pamphlets are listed:

BOOKS

BOLUS, MALVINA, ed., *Image of Canada.* Toronto: Ryerson, 1953.

BROWN, G. W., *Canada* (United Nations Series). Berkeley: University of California Press, 1950.

BUCHANAN, DONALD, ed., *This Is Canada.* Toronto: Ryerson, 1945.

CARELESS, J. M. S., *Canada: A Story of Challenge.* New York: Cambridge University Press, 1953.

CARNEGIE SERIES, *The Relations of Canada and the United States.* New Haven: Yale University Press; Toronto: Ryerson, 1936–1945.

EGGLESTON, WILFRED, *The Road to Nationhood.* New York: Oxford University Press, 1946.

MCINNIS, EDGAR, *Canada: A Political and Social History.* Toronto: Clarke, Irwin Co., Ltd., 1947.

MCRAE, D. G. W., *The Arts and Crafts of Canada.* New York: Macmillan, 1944.

ROBERTS, LESLIE, *Canada: The Golden Hinge.* New York: Rinehart & Co., Inc., 1952.

SANDWELL, B. K., *The Canadian Peoples.* New York: Oxford University Press, 1947.

PAMPHLETS

BROWN, G. W., *Canadian Democracy in Action.* Toronto: J. M. Dent & Sons, Ltd., 1945.

Canada Handbook Annual. Ottawa: Queen's Printer.

Canada: Descriptive Atlas. Ottawa: Queen's Printer.

PROVINCIAL ASPECT SERIES (a series of 10 pamphlets, one for each province, entitled *The Province of Newfoundland, The Province of Nova Scotia,* etc.). Ottawa: The Canadian Geographical Society, 1948.